Did Y

BERK

A MISCELLANY

Compiled by Julia Skinner

With particular reference to the work of Martin Andrew
and Nick Channer

THE FRANCIS FRITH COLLECTION

www.francisfrith.com

First published in the United Kingdom in 2011 by The Francis Frith Collection®

This edition published exclusively for Identity Books in 2012 ISBN 978-1-84589-577-8

British Library Cataloguing in Publication Data

Did You Know? Berkshire - A Miscellany
Compiled by Julia Skinner
With particular reference to the work of Martin Andrew and Nick Channer

The Francis Frith Collection
Oakley Business Park,
Wylye Road, Dinton,
Wiltshire SP3 5EU
Tel: +44 (0) 1722 716 376
Email: info@francisfrith.co.uk
www.francisfrith.com

Printed and bound in Malaysia

Front Cover: **MAIDENHEAD, CLIVEDEN WOODS 1925** 77613p
Frontispiece: **READING, MARKET PLACE 1870** R13001

The colour-tinting is for illustrative purposes only, and is not intended to be historically accurate

CONTENTS

INTRODUCTION

The name of Berkshire means 'the district of wooded hills'. Small though it is, Berkshire is packed with history. With its gentle beauty and rich, varied landscape ranging from sweeping open downland with far-reaching views, woodlands and parks, to winding rivers and attractive villages, it is hardly surprising that visitors and residents alike are drawn to its numerous charms.

Berkshire really consists of two distinct parts. The western half is essentially rural and undeveloped – racing country. Here, the Lambourn Downs sweep down to the pretty River Lambourn, and the Berkshire Downs to the majestic River Thames. Between the M4 and A4, near Newbury, there are areas of delightful woodland and common land where pretty villages nestle among the trees and open spaces. The eastern half of Berkshire is quite different, with an awesome concentration of housing, as well as industrial and commercial development. In recent years towns like Slough, Maidenhead, Bracknell, Wokingham and Reading have encroached on the surrounding countryside, and we have to look hard to find truly unspoilt pockets of peace and tranquillity. But they are there, providing refuge from the urban jungle if we are prepared to look for them.

Stone Age, Bronze Age and Iron Age people all lived within the county and left their stamp on Berkshire, and burial mounds and Iron Age hill-forts are scattered over the landscape. After the fall of the Roman Empire, the invading Anglo-Saxons wrestled the Berkshire area from the Romano-Britons in the sixth century; then two Saxon kingdoms, Mercia and Wessex, battled for possession of it. After the Norman Conquest of 1066, William the Conqueror established the first castle at Windsor; the huge and impressive fortress that stands there now is one of Britain's iconic buildings. The Normans also left their mark in some of the county's churches; one of the most interesting is the church of St James at Finchampstead, with a Norman nave, chancel and circular-shaped sanctuary, a rare feature in English churches. Other notable examples of Norman work are the church of St Mark and St Luke at Avington near Kintbury, the church of St Michael and All Angels at Lambourn, and the church of Saint Laurence at Upton-cum-Chalvey, the oldest building in what is now the borough of Slough.

Berkshire witnessed great activity in the wool and cloth trade between the Middle Ages and the 17th century, with Newbury and Reading being particularly important centres. From the late 18th century the map of Berkshire gradually changed as various transport systems threaded their way across the county, which greatly affected the county's trade and industry. What is now the A4 was established as the Bath Road, which was significantly improved by the introduction of turnpike trusts. Coaching inns lined its route, and towns and villages in the vicinity of the road grew in size and importance. Running parallel to the Bath Road through Berkshire in the 19th century were the Kennet and Avon Canal, which cut through the heart of west Berkshire, and Brunel's Great Western Railway, which crossed the county towards Bristol. In the 20th century Berkshire witnessed even greater changes as new roads and motorways began to spring up everywhere, and the population of the county increased dramatically as thousands of new homes were built within its boundaries.

Before 1974, much of what is now south Oxfordshire was part of Berkshire, including the towns of Wantage, Wallingford and Abingdon, which used to be the county town; however, Reading effectively became the county town in 1867 when the summer assizes were moved there from Abingdon, and this was made official in 1869. Following the Local Government Act of 1972, the whole of the Vale of the White Horse was transferred from Berkshire to Oxfordshire in 1974. Often known as the Royal County of Berkshire because of the presence of the royal residence of Windsor Castle, in the 1990s Berkshire was divided into unitary authorities within a county council administration.

BERKSHIRE DIALECT
WORDS AND PHRASES

'Cheeselog' - a woodlouse.

'Deedy' - careful.

'Dout' - to put out a fire.

'Footer' - to cry.

'Shucketty' - shaky.

'Pikked' - pointed.

'Bottom' - a valley.

'Tarblish' - tolerable.

'Snook' - stolen.

'Wuut' - a mole.

'Veatish' - healthy.

'Vorights' - opposite.

WARGRAVE, THE VILLAGE 1890 27177

HAUNTED BERKSHIRE

There are a number of haunted locations in Berkshire. Here are two of the most famous:

Bisham Abbey in the north of the county is a Tudor mansion that was built by the Hoby family incorporating the remains of a Benedictine abbey. It is reputed to be haunted by the ghost of Dame Elizabeth, the wife of Sir Thomas Hoby who completed the building of the house (she later married Lord Russell after Sir Thomas's death in 1566). Legend says that she beat her son William so hard for not attending to his studies and blotting his copybook that he died as a result; she was overcome with remorse for the rest of her life and her guilt-ridden ghost haunts the house, trying to wash her bloodstained hands in a ghostly basin. Her apparition is said to emerge from her portrait hanging in the Great Hall and then roam the building, being particularly active in the East Wing. Dame Elizabeth died in 1609, and she has an impressive alabaster tomb in the Hoby Chapel of Bisham's parish church of All Saints. Her effigy shows her kneeling in widow's weeds under a canopy with Corinthian columns. Behind her are her deceased children (three daughters and a son), and outside the columns kneel the daughter and two sons who survived her.

Windsor Castle is said to be roamed by a number of royal ghosts. Amongst them are the black-gowned shade of Queen Elizabeth I which has been seen many times in the Royal Library (this was part of the State Apartments in Tudor times), and the ghost of Henry VIII's first wife, Catherine of Aragon, which is reputed to visit the Queen's Closet, overlooking the Quire in St George's Chapel. Henry VIII himself may haunt the Dean's Cloister area, where ghostly groans and shuffling footsteps have been heard; there have also been reported sightings of a mysterious bulky figure there, which is assumed to be the king's ghost – two soldiers reported seeing it in 1977, and described how it seemed to fade away into a wall…

BERKSHIRE MISCELLANY

We start our tour around Berkshire at Lambourn, amidst the Lambourn Downs in the north-west of the county. The name of 'Lambourn' probably originates from when sheep were dipped in the local stream, or 'bourn'. Nowadays, this area is famous as 'The Valley of the Racehorse'; the well-drained open downland around the village is ideal for training racehorses and this is one of the main training areas in the country, with around 1,500 horses stabled locally. Lambourn's parish church of St Michael and All Angels is mainly Norman but was much restored in the 19th century. Amongst the monuments in the church is a memorial brass to John Estbury (died 1508), who founded the Estbury (or Istbury) Almshouses outside the church for ten elderly poor men in 1502. The almshouses were rebuilt in the 19th century into the form we see today – the building with a tower of patterned brickwork on the right hand side of photograph L530023, below. The churchyard contains the grave of John Carter, who in 1832 burned down the Red Lion Inn in Lambourn and was the last man to be hanged for arson in Britain. The inscription on his headstone tells his story.

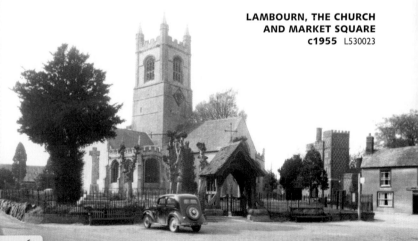

**LAMBOURN, THE CHURCH
AND MARKET SQUARE
c1955** L530023

The River Lambourn is a chalk stream that rises in the downs near Lambourn and flows south-east through the Lambourn Valley to join the River Kennet near the village of Shaw, north of Newbury. Along its course is the village of Eastbury. Its parish church of St James the Greater features a beautiful engraved-glass window by Laurence Whistler dedicated to the poet Edward Thomas (1878-1917) who died in the First World War, and his wife Helen, who lived at Bridge Cottage in the village from 1954 until her death in 1967. Their daughter Myfanwy commissioned the window in memory of her parents. Donations to pay for the work were received from all over the world by admirers of Edward Thomas's poetry, some lines of which feature in the artwork.

Also along the course of the River Lambourn are two villages that have the only two round-towered churches in Berkshire, St Mary's at Great Shefford and St Gregory's at Welford, north-west of Newbury.

Another interesting church in this area is St Swithin's at Wickham, north-west of Newbury. It has a sturdy Saxon tower that is believed to be the oldest church tower in Berkshire. Originally it seems to have had a dual purpose as a look-out tower or tower of refuge, since there is a doorway high up the building that would have accessed by a ladder that was then pulled up inside, and there are also slots for beams which may have supported warning beacons. The interior of the church is notable for the set of eight extraordinary and brightly coloured papier-mâché elephants' heads in full ceremonial dress that appear to support the beams of the north aisle roof, giving the church the appearance of an Indian temple. They were put in the church by a 19th-century rector, Reverend William Nicholson, who saw them at the Paris Exhibition of 1862. He originally bought a few of the heads to embellish the rectory, but decided to use them in the church instead, commissioning more to be made to complete the set.

HUNGERFORD, HIGH STREET 1903 49383

On the western edge of the county, close to the border with Wiltshire, is Hungerford, which had become a borough by 1131, with a market charter of 1296 granted by Edward III; by the 17th century its market was an important centre for sheep, cattle and wool. Photograph 49383 (above) of its High Street shows the wide street that was typical of many country towns in the past, designed so that markets could be held without blocking the thoroughfare. The ornately-decorated Victorian Town Hall and Corn Exchange on the right of the picture, with its gigantic clock tower, dates from 1870.

In 1688, it was at the Bear Hotel in Charnham Street in Hungerford that the Protestant Dutchman William of Orange accepted the throne of England, after deposing his father-in-law, the Catholic King James II, in the Glorious Revolution – so called because little blood was spilt. The only significant fighting of the Glorious Revolution also took place in Berkshire, when King James's army was defeated and put to flight by William's forces near Reading. William and his wife Mary subsequently became the monarchs King William III and Queen Mary II.

The River Kennet that runs through Hungerford was once described as 'a fayre river which yieldeth store of fishes and especiallie trowtes'. In the 14th century the people of Hungerford were granted special fishing and grazing rights by the lord of the manor, John of Gaunt (a son of Edward III), who also gave the town a brass drinking-horn that is kept in the town hall. The award of these rights is still celebrated in Hungerford as part of the annual Hocktide Festival on the second Tuesday after Easter. Hocktide used to be observed all over the country, but Hungerford is now the only place where this old custom is held. Hocktide in the spring and Michaelmas in the autumn traditionally divided the rural year into its winter and summer halves. As the beginning of the 'summer' half, Hocktide was a good excuse for a celebration. Hungerford's Hocktide Festival begins with the town crier blowing a replica of John of Gaunt's horn summoning residents of the town with commoners' rights to the Hocktide Court in the town hall, where they pay rents to safeguard their rights of fishing and grazing. Two 'Tutti-Men' are then elected and given 'tutti poles' decorated with ribbons and posies of flowers ('tutti' is an old word for a posy). The Tutti-Men, smartly dressed in top hat and tails, are then led through the town accompanied by the 'Orange-Man' and are entitled to claim a kiss from all the women resident in the town, who receive an orange in return.

Hungerford's prosperity was helped by the opening of the Kennet & Avon Canal in 1810, which linked the Thames to the Bristol Channel via the existing Kennet and Avon river navigations. Like many canals its business suffered in competition against the railways, and by the 1950s it was sliding into dereliction. Canal enthusiasts successfully fought against its closure and mobilised a huge voluntary effort to help British Waterways restore it. In 1990 the whole 57 miles (91.7km) of its route again became navigable, and was reopened. The Kennet & Avon Canal is now used for boating, and walking and cycling are enjoyed along its towpath.

East of Hungerford, the Kennet & Avon Canal meets the River Kennet at Newbury. Newbury Lock (Lock 85), near the Lock, Stock & Barrel pub in Northbrook Street, was the first lock to be built on the canal (in 1796) and was also the only lock on the canal to use 'Jack Cloughs' – manually operated ground paddles that are levered open. The 'Jack Cloughs' can still be seen at Newbury Lock, although they are not used nowadays as the lock also has gate paddles.

The name of Newbury means 'New Borough', and the town was probably founded by the lord of the manor, Arnulf de Hesdin, in the 1070s to develop commerce and trade in the area. Newbury's wealth was based on the wool and cloth trade from the Middle Ages until the late 16th century. Another local industry was recorded by the traveller Celia Fiennes, who visited Newbury in 1698 and said that it was 'a little town famous for makeing the best whipps'.

NEWBURY, MARKET PLACE 1952 N61024

Medieval Newbury's most famous inhabitant was John Winchcombe, known as Jack O'Newbury, 'the richest clothier England ever beheld'. He employed over 1,000 people in a medieval cloth 'factory' with over 200 looms, which extended from his home in Northbrook Street to where Victoria Park is now. Marks & Spencer now stands on the site of John Winchcombe's home. Only one gable end of his house survives (in Marsh Lane), but it is an important example of 16th-century brick and timber architecture, including a fine oriel window. It was John Winchcombe who started the building of Newbury's magnificent St Nicolas's Church; it is one of Berkshire's finest 'wool churches', meaning it was built from the profits of the wool and cloth industry. He died in 1519 and the church was completed by his son, also called John. There is a fine memorial brass to John Winchcombe the elder (and Alice, his first wife) beneath the tower, which shows him wearing a long fur-lined cloak, with a purse hanging from his belt.

The decline of Newbury's wool and cloth trade caused much hardship in the town, and the Cloth Hall in Wharf Street was built in the 17th century to provide unemployed weavers with work. It now forms part of the West Berkshire Museum, together with the old Granary nearby. An exhibition in the museum tells the story of the famous Newbury Coat. In 1811 a bet of a thousand guineas was made between Sir John Throckmorton and John Coxeter, a local cloth manufacturer, on whether a gentleman's coat could be produced in a single day, from the shearing of the wool from the sheep at 5am through to the wearing of the finished coat at 8pm. The feat was attempted near Greenham Mills in front of 5,000 people, and a 'well woven, properly made coat' was presented to Sir John at 6.20pm, with nearly two hours to spare. In 1991 the feat was attempted again at the Newbury Show, and the garment was produced in the same way but beat the time by one hour; this coat is on display in the West Berkshire Museum, together with items relating to the making of the original Newbury Coat of 1811, which is kept in the Throckmorton family home at Coughton Court in Warwickshire.

The Newbury area was the scene of two major battles during the Civil War. The First Battle of Newbury was fought in September 1643 south of the town in the Wash Common area. Wash Common is now a suburb of Newbury and some of its roads are named after leaders of both sides in the battle, such as Charles Street, after King Charles I, Essex Street, after the Parliamentarian Earl of Essex, and Falkland Road, after the Royalist Viscount Falkland who was killed in the bloody encounter, along with around 6,000 others. The Second Battle of Newbury took place in October 1644 at Speen, north of the town. The battle was inconclusive but the Royalist army was able to slip away, leaving the royal crown, the Great Seal and the artillery in the keeping of Colonel Boys at nearby Donnington Castle. The Parliamentarians then besieged the castle, but Colonel Boys did not surrender until instructed by the king to do so, in April 1646. Most of the castle was then demolished by order of Parliament, but the outline of the fortress is still visible, and its magnificent 14th-century gatehouse still stands, seen in photograph N61008a, below.

**NEWBURY
DONNINGTON CASTLE
c1955** N61008a

East of Newbury is Thatcham. Inside its parish church of St Mary is the tomb of Francis Baily (1774-1844), a local man who was a founder member of the Astronomical Society and later became its president. He discovered 'Baily's beads' – gaseous particles in the sun's corona. He also carried out experiments to determine the weight and density of the earth. He is commemorated in the name of the Francis Baily Primary School in Thatcham.

South-east of Thatcham is Aldermaston, equidistant between Newbury and Reading. The village is famous for a local custom that dates from 1815 – every three years a candle auction is held in the parish hall, when people bid for the lease-rights to a 2-acre plot of local land owned by the Church, known as Church Acre. A horseshoe nail is driven into the side of a candle, which is then lit. Bidding takes place until the candle burns down far enough for the nail to fall out, and the winning bid is the last one to be made before this happens. The rent money so obtained is used for charitable purposes.

Another historic local custom takes place at Ufton Nervet, north-east of Aldermaston, where local parishioners can claim their Ufton Bread Dole every Maundy Thursday (the day before Good Friday, at Easter). The tradition began in 1581 when the Elizabethan manor house of Ufton Court in the village was the home of Lady Marvyn. The story goes that she once got lost in local woodland, and was so grateful to the villagers who rescued her that she left money in her will for an annual dole of wheat, canvas and cloth to be given to the 'poore of Upton'. The custom has been upheld by the landlords of Ufton Court ever since, and local residents of the parish of Ufton Nervet still queue up outside a window of Ufton Court on Maundy Thursday to claim their dole, which now comprises two loaves of bread per person, whilst some people are also entitled to a white towel.

Our tour now moves to Reading, Berkshire's county town. Reading's fine Town Hall in Blagrave Street was designed in Gothic style by the famous architect and Reading resident Alfred Waterhouse, and built in 1875 (photograph 31720, above). Reading Borough Council is now based in a modern Civic Centre in Castle Street, and the Town Hall is used as a cultural centre and home of the Museum of Reading. One of the museum's treasures is a full-sized replica of the Bayeux Tapestry that was made in the 1880s by the Leek Embroidery Society in Staffordshire. It was bought for the town in 1895 by Arthur Hill, a former Mayor of Reading, and is displayed in its own gallery.

Blagrave Street in Reading is named after the famous mathematician John Blagrave, born locally in 1561 and educated at Reading School, who published four influential books on mathematics. He died in 1611 and was buried in St Laurence's Church in Reading (on the right of photograph 31720, above). There is an interesting monument to him on the south wall of the church, showing him surrounded by geometric symbols.

Reading's prosperity in the Middle Ages owed much to its wool and cloth trade, and an old tradition connects a Reading cloth merchant with a measure of length. According to the tale, during the reign of Henry I (1100-1135) one of the richest cloth merchants in England was a man known as 'Thomas of Reading'. One day the king and his party met Thomas and his fellow merchants on the road, but their many wagons forced the royal party to move aside. At first King Henry was angry, but then he realised how useful the support of such rich men might be; to win their favour, he established a standard measurement for cloth – the yard, which was exactly the length of his arm.

Henry I has another connection with Reading, for in 1121 he founded an abbey in the town that was also his place of burial in 1136. Reading Abbey was one of the richest and most powerful houses in England until the monasteries were dissolved by Henry VIII. In 1539 its last abbot, Hugh Faringdon, was executed because he would not acknowledge the king's supremacy over the Pope, and the abbey was closed down and mostly demolished. On a wall of the abbey ruins next to Forbury Gardens a plaque displays the words and music for the earliest recorded English song, which was written down at Reading Abbey in the 1240s – the harmony round 'Sumer is icumen in' (Summer is a-coming in), also known as the 'Reading Rota'. The original manuscript is in the British Library. The only complete survival from the abbey is its splendid gateway that led into the monastic precincts, seen in the background of photograph 64639 on page 16.

Medieval England was famous for its archers, and it was compulsory for all adult males to practice their longbow skills every Sunday. Reading's men practiced on land in front of St Mary's Church, where archery 'butts' (practice fields and targets), were set up, which is how the street of St Mary's Butts got its name. Fifty archers from Reading went to France with King Henry V and helped win the battle of Agincourt in 1415.

READING, SUTTON'S SEEDS 1912 64639

Reading was once famous for its three Bs – beer (Simonds Brewery, makers of India Pale Ale), bulbs (Sutton Seeds, which moved to Torquay in 1974) and biscuits (Huntley & Palmer). The Huntley & Palmer works on Kings Road employed over 5,000 people, giving Reading and its football club the nicknames of 'The Biscuit Town' and 'The Biscuit Men'. Founded in 1822 by Thomas Huntley, who went into partnership with George Palmer in 1841, Huntley & Palmer revolutionised biscuit manufacture by putting their products into decorative tins, which solved the problem of keeping them fresh. After various company mergers Huntley & Palmer's production moved to Liverpool in 1976, and the Reading works was demolished. All that remains is its old social club, now converted to housing.

The Huntley & Palmer works was close to Reading Gaol, where the author and playwright Oscar Wilde was imprisoned for 2 years in the 1890s for homosexual offences. The execution of one of the inmates during Wilde's time there, for murdering his wife, inspired his poem 'The Ballad of Reading Gaol' of 1898.

Photograph 2865 (below) shows Broad Street in Reading around 1905, with the statue of George Palmer of the Huntley & Palmer biscuit company in pride of place – it now stands in Palmer Park, laid out in the 1880s on land given to the town by Mr Palmer. It is an unusual statue, showing the biscuit baron holding an umbrella and silk hat.

In the 19th century Reading was famous for a local condiment, 'Reading Sauce'. This was described as a sharp sauce flavoured with onion, spices and herbs, much like Worcestershire sauce. It featured in Jules Verne's novel 'Around the World in Eighty Days' of 1873, in which the hero Phileas Fogg enjoys 'a side dish, a boiled fish with Reading sauce of first quality'.

Reading features in Thomas Hardy's novel 'Jude the Obscure', disguised under the fictional name of 'Aldbrickham', where Jude and Sue lived and ran a monumental masonry business. Newbury also appears in the book, as 'Kennetbridge', where Jude came to visit the composer of a hymn.

**READING
BROAD STREET
c1905** 2865

At the centre of Reading's Market Place is the Simeon Monument, designed by Sir John Soane and erected in 1804 (see photograph R13001 on the title page). The stone obelisk supported three gas lanterns to light the market place at night, and was given to the town by Edward Simeon, a wealthy banker, former Director of the Bank of England and Mayor of Reading, 'as a mark of affection to his native town'. It has been restored in recent years, and the original gas lanterns have been replaced with electric replicas.

One of Reading's landmarks is Caversham Bridge, connecting the town centre with Caversham on the other side of the Thames, which flows north of the town. Caversham was in Oxfordshire until 1911. Part of the 'deal' whereby Oxfordshire surrendered Caversham to the borough of Reading was the rebuilding of the 1869 bridge seen in photograph 59962, below, which was found to be sub-standard and was replaced by the present concrete one in 1926.

CAVERSHAM, BRIDGE STREET 1908 59962

North-west of Reading is Pangbourne, where the River Pang converges with the Thames. A privately-owned toll bridge famous for its cast iron lattice design spans the Thames here. The name of Pangbourne means 'Paega's People's Stream', showing that this area was settled by an early Saxon leader and his followers. The village sign depicts a Saxon ship and Berhtwulf, the Saxon King of Mercia, holding the village charter – he was given land at Pangbourne in AD 844 by the Bishop of Leicester in return for a grant of liberties for some monasteries. The sign also features an open book and some trees, a reference to Kenneth Graham, author 'The Wind in the Willows', who retired to Church Cottage in Pangbourne and lived there until his death in 1932. He did not write the book in Pangbourne (see page 21), but the riverside scenery along the Thames in the area is said to have inspired E H Shepherd's illustrations for the book.

Further up the Thames from Pangbourne is Lower Basildon, the birthplace in 1674 of Jethro Tull, 'the father of mechanised farming'. He disliked the laborious manual work involved in farming in those days, and invented a horse-drawn seed drill for sowing crops and a horse-drawn hoe for clearing weeds, to make farm work easier, faster and more efficient. He perfected his ideas at Prosperous Farm near Hungerford, where he moved in 1709. He died there in 1741, but was buried in St Bartholomew's churchyard at Lower Basildon; his resting place is marked with a gravestone featuring a carved image of one of his horse-drawn machines. (The gravestone incorrectly dates his death as 1740.)

Close to Lower Basildon is the National Trust property of Basildon Park, which was used as a location for Netherfield Park in the 2005 feature film of 'Pride and Prejudice'. In 1911 some of the directors of the London stationary firm of Millington & Sons were staying at Basildon Park. They were about to launch a new range of writing paper, but had not yet found a name for it. They decided to use the name of the house where they were staying for the new brand, which became famous as Basildon Bond.

Our tour now moves back to the Reading area, and follows the Thames eastwards from Caversham to Sonning, where the river is crossed by a redbrick 18th-century bridge with eleven arches. In the centre of the bridge is a stone marker inscribed 'B | O', showing the position of the county boundary between Berkshire and Oxfordshire – the vertical line indicates where the boundary runs down the middle of the river. The house known as 'Turpins' at the corner of Sonning Lane and Pearson Road, near the gates of Home Park, was the home in the 18th century of an aunt of the notorious highwayman Dick Turpin (1705-1739). There used to be an underground stable below the house (now blocked up), which was accessed by a ramp. Legend says that Dick Turpin would hide his horse there after carrying out a hold-up on the Bath Road and then go into hiding from his pursuers until it was safe to come back to retrieve his horse.

East of Sonning is Twyford. William Penn, the founder of the American state of Pennsylvania, lived near the town at Ruscombe from 1710 until his death in 1718. He is commemorated in Twyford in the name of a residential street, 'Pennfields'.

The Thames flows out of Berkshire near Wargrave, heading to Henley-on-Thames. Then the river flows along the northern border of the county in a loop around Maidenhead. One of the Thames-side villages north of Maidenhead is Cookham, famous as the birthplace and home of the quirky artist Sir Stanley Spencer, RA (1891-1959). Stanley Spencer was born in 'Fernlea', a house in the High Street close to the King's Arms Hotel, and lived there for much of his eccentric life. He featured many Cookham locations and people in his work, including the churchyard where he set his Resurrection painting. More than 100 of his paintings and drawings can be seen in The Stanley Spencer Gallery in Cookham, housed in the former Methodist chapel at the east end of the High Street.

The author Kenneth Grahame spent part of his childhood in Cookham Dean at his grandmother's home, a country house called The Mount, and he came back with his wife and son in 1906 to live at 'Mayfield' on Dean Lane, now the Herries school. He wrote much of 'The Wind in the Willows' there, influenced by the scenery along the Thames. The nearby woods at Bisham are believed to have inspired the Wild Wood of the book.

Many people come to Cookham to see the local stage of a ceremony called 'Swan Upping', although this can also be watched in other parts of Berkshire along the course of the Thames. Swan Upping is carried out every year over five days during the third week of July, along a 70-mile stretch of the Thames between Sunbury on Thames in Surrey and Abingdon in Oxfordshire. The mute swans on the Thames officially belong either to the Crown or the two historic livery companies of the Vintners and Dyers, and during Swan Upping the new cygnets are counted and their ownership is assigned. Swan Upping is a colourful event involving the Swan Marker, 19 Swan Uppers, the Swan Warden and teams from the two livery companies, all dressed in their respective uniforms. The Swan Uppers progress along the Thames in their skiffs, looking for swans and their cygnets. When a flock of swans is found, the Uppers form a corral of skiffs around the birds and lift them out of the water. In this way they can make notes on their state of health, and weigh and measure them, so the ceremony also serves as a census and health check. If the parents of a cygnet have Vintners' or Dyers' rings, then the cygnets are also ringed to show which livery company they belong to, and the ownership is recorded. If the parents are not ringed, they belong to the Crown and so do the cygnets. After this, the birds are put back into the river and the Swan Uppers move on upstream.

Maidenhead's position at a crossing over the Thames is the key to its growth and development. Originally Maidenhead was based on North Town, but another settlement developed where the main road from London crossed the Thames by ferry half a mile to the east. By the late 13th century a timber bridge had replaced the ferry, and the settlement beside it based its trade on tolls collected from traffic using the bridge. The name of this settlement became 'Maidenhythe' – referring to the new, or 'maiden', hythe, or wharf, over the Thames. The modern spelling of 'Maidenhead' first appears in Tudor times. The elegant sandstone bridge that now carries the A4 road over the Thames at Maidenhead was built in the 1770s, and remained a toll bridge until 1903 when the tolls were abolished.

By the mid 18th century Maidenhead had become a busy staging post on the London to Bath road, and its main street was lined with coaching inns. Many coaches stopped at Maidenhead to rest up overnight before tackling the steep Castle Hill and the dangers of Maidenhead Thicket, two miles west of the town centre. This area was a notorious haunt of thieves, footpads and highwaymen until well into the 19th century, and not a pleasant area to travel through at night.

Castle Hill takes the Bath Road (A4) out of Maidenhead. It was formerly called Folly Hill, but was renamed Castle Hill after the Windsor Castle Inn up the hill, so named because Windsor Castle could be seen from there. Those who climb Castle Hill nowadays will notice two curious old buildings halfway up. On the south side is a mock castle, known as Castle Hill Folly, which was built in 1897 as a quirky house. The other building on the north side, a three-storey house with a first floor verandah and arched windows on the top storey, was originally built around 1890 as an ice house for a local fishmonger. It was constructed over two deep vaulted brick wells that were filled with ice from the winter-frozen Moor Stream, providing ice all the year round to keep his fish fresh.

As well as being famous for its graceful 1770s river bridge, Maidenhead is also renowned for its railway bridge, designed by Isambard Kingdom Brunel for the Great Western Railway and completed in 1838. Brunel crossed the Thames with two immense, almost flat, brick-arched spans, each 39 metres (128 feet) across with a rise of only 7.3 metres (24 feet). The bridge was an extraordinary engineering feat, and its remarkable two arches remain the widest and flattest brick arches in the world. A dramatic echo can be experienced when standing on the path beneath the bridge, giving it the name of the 'Sounding Arch'. In 1854 the bridge was portrayed by the artist J M W Turner in a painting titled 'Rain, Steam and Speed', which hangs in the National Gallery in London.

The coming of the railway in the 19th century destroyed Maidenhead's coaching trade but brought new opportunities. Maidenhead also benefited from the boating boom of the late 19th century, as the Thames became a waterway increasingly orientated towards leisure. A number of prestigious hotels were built and Maidenhead became a fashionable riverside resort town, with a Promenade along the river bank.

MAIDENHEAD, THE HIGH STREET AND THE TOWN HALL 1903 50833

Photograph 50833 (above) shows Maidenhead's High Street in the early 20th century. The building with the pillars on the left of the view was its 18th-century Town Hall, which was given a Victorian make-over in 1878-80. This Town Hall was demolished in 1962 and replaced by Berkshire House, a three-storey block with a further nine-storey office tower above. A new Town Hall was built in 1962 in St Ives Road, now the headquarters of the Royal Borough of Windsor and Maidenhead Council – eagle-eyed movie buffs may recognise the building masquerading as a hospital in some of the 'Carry On' films. Much of the old historic fabric of Maidenhead was demolished in the 1960s and replaced with modern buildings or new road systems. One of the town's best modern buildings is the stylish library of 1973, also in St Ives Road, which is already a protected building. The government added it to the Statutory List of Buildings of Special Architectural or Historic Interest in 2003 as Grade II. An important building, designed by one of the leading architects of the time, Paul Koralek of Ahrends, Burton and Koralek, it joins a select band of modern listed buildings.

A Victorian traveller alighting from a train at Maidenhead Railway Station today would recognise little from the present town, but one landmark that would be familiar is the Clock Tower at the south end of King Street near the station, built to commemorate Queen Victoria's Diamond Jubilee of 1897. The present-day traveller alighting at platform three of the station passes an intriguing statue of a man sitting on a bench holding an open book. The work, by local sculptor Lydia Karpinska, commemorates Maidenhead resident Sir Nicholas Winton, dubbed the 'British Schindler' for smuggling 669 Jewish children out of Czechoslovakia in 1939 when Nazi invasion of the country was imminent, thus saving them from Nazi concentration camps. The children were taken in by British families found by Sir Nicholas, who agreed to fund the cost of evacuating them and look after them until they were 17. Sir Nicholas made his home at Pinkneys Green later in his life and became a member of the Maidenhead Rotary Club and a supporter of several local organisations and charities. Aged 101, he attended the unveiling of the statue in 2010, which shows him reading a book containing images of some of the children he saved.

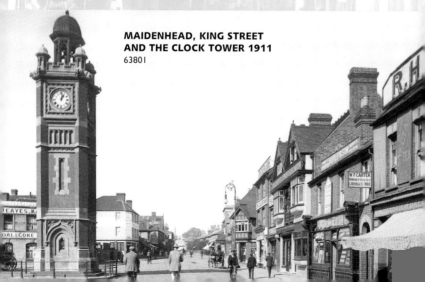

MAIDENHEAD, KING STREET AND THE CLOCK TOWER 1911
63801

South-east of Maidenhead is the Thames-side village of Bray which is famous for a ballad about its vicar who regularly changed his religion to avoid losing his desirable living: 'Whatsoever King shall reign, I will always be the Vicar of Bray, Sir!'. The song is believed to refer to Simon Alleyn, who was Vicar of Bray from 1540 to 1588, through the reigns of Henry VIII and his three children, Edward VI, Mary I and Elizabeth I, and who was twice a Catholic and twice a Protestant during that time of turbulent political and religious change. Nowadays Bray is also famous as the location of Heston Blumenthal's Fat Duck Restaurant, renowned for its menu of unusual dishes such as 'snail porridge' and 'bacon and egg ice-cream'. They must taste better than they sound, for the restaurant has been named the Best Restaurant in the UK a number of times in recent years by the Good Food Guide.

Downriver from Bray is Monkey Island. A fishing lodge was built on the island for the Duke of Marlborough in the 1740s in which a room was painted by the noted artist Andieu de Clermont as a 'singerie', with scenes of monkeys fishing, shooting and following outdoor sports. Now known as the Monkey Room, the former fishing lodge is now part of the Monkey Island Hotel.

What is now the Oakley Court Hotel in Windsor Road at Water Oakley near Bray was built as a mansion house in full-blown Victorian Gothic style in the mid 19th century. Oakley Court was used as a setting for a number of films made in the 1960s and 70s at Bray Studios, based next door at Down Place. The distinctive and dramatic-looking building featured most notably in the films made by Hammer House Productions, and appeared as Dracula's castle in 'The Brides of Dracula'; it was also used as the location of Frank N Furter's castle in the film of 'The Rocky Horror Picture Show'.

SLOUGH, HIGH STREET c1960 S256068

Now in Berkshire, but formerly in Buckinghamshire, Slough dates back to the 12th century, when it was a hamlet on the London to Bath road. Positioned at the crossroads of that road and a north-south route from Berkhamsted to Windsor, Slough developed as a coaching town in the 18th century and expanded greatly after the Great Western Railway arrived in the 19th century. The A4 passed through the High Street until the early 1970s. Slough began to expand into the large modern town we know today in the 1920s, after Slough Estates acquired 700 acres of derelict land in the area and created the Slough Trading Estate, which at the time was considered enterprising and innovative. John Betjeman's famous lines of 1937, 'Come, friendly bombs, and fall on Slough, It isn't fit for humans now. There isn't grass to graze a cow', were rather unfair. Slough Estates gradually transformed a scruffy area into a prosperous trading estate that helped develop a thriving town. Indeed, the poet's daughter, Candida Lycett-Green, apologised for the poem on a visit to Slough in 2006 and said that her father had regretted having written it and had never wanted it published.

SLOUGH, WILLIAM STREET
1961 S256070

One of Slough's earliest industries was brickmaking. Bricks were being made in the area at least as early as 1442, when records show that the first consignment of 2,500,000 Slough-made bricks were delivered for the building of Eton College (see page 30). In the 19th century the main brickfields were located in the Langley and Upton Lea areas, but brickmaking in Slough ceased in the mid 20th century and the brickfields have now been redeveloped as housing or industrial estates.

Another famous local industry in Slough's story was started in the mid 19th century by James Elliman. Originally he had a draper's business in Chandos Street, but in 1847 he also began to sell his 'Elliman's Embrocation', a muscle rub, and a similar product for horses, 'Royal Embrocation' horse liniment. These products proved so successful that he closed his drapery business and concentrated on manufacturing them commercially from factories in Chandos Street and Wellington Street. James Elliman became a major benefactor to the town, and is remembered today in the names of Elliman Avenue and the James Elliman Primary School. Ellimans Universal Embrocation is still made, but is now manufactured by GlaxoSmithKline.

Herschell Street in Slough is named after the astronomer Sir William Herschell (1738-1822), who is also commemorated in the town with a monument in Windsor Road. Sir William Herschell came to live in Slough in 1786 and remained there for the rest of his life. The modern office block called Observatory House at the corner of Herschell Street and Windsor Road is built on the site of the house where he lived, and where he erected a giant 40-foot telescope in the garden. The telescope had a 48 inch mirror, and observations he made with it helped him make the first true map of the universe. Herschell had previously (1781) discovered a 'new' planet, which he named 'The Georgian' in honour of King George III – we now know it as Uranus. This discovery doubled the size of the solar system as it was then known. Whilst living at Slough, Herschell discovered 2 new moons orbiting Saturn. In 1788 he married his wife Mary Pitt at St Laurence's Church at Upton-cum-Chalvey, which was also his burial place after his death in 1822. His Latin epitaph in the church translates as 'William Herschell, Knight of the Guelphic Order, born at Hanover, he chose England for his country. Amongst the most Distinguished Astronomers of his age he was deservedly reckoned. For should his lesser discoveries be passed over, he was the first man to discover a planet outside the orbit of Saturn, aided by new contrivances he himself both invented and constructed.' Herschell is also commemorated in the church with a beautiful stained glass window, showing him at his telescope observing a night sky full of planets.

One of Britain's favourite apple varieties was developed at Colnbrook near Slough (then in Buckinghamshire but now in Berkshire) in the 1820s, when Richard Cox planted a seed from a Ribston Pippin which he pollinated with a Blenheim Orange. Cox's Orange Pippin is now the most important British dessert apple, accounting for three quarters of all dessert apples grown in the country.

ETON, THE COLLEGE CHAPEL FROM BARNES POOL BRIDGE 1914
67007

South of Slough is Eton, on the north bank of the Thames. In 1440 King Henry VI decided to found a splendid church at Eton, attached to which would be a college of ten priests and a school for 25 poor scholars. Eton College chapel (built between 1449 and 1482) was originally planned to form the choir of the church, but the rest of the building project was dropped after Henry VI was deposed in 1461. The chapel is seen in the background of photograph 67007 (above), whilst boys from Eton College stroll along the road in their distinctive uniform of black tailcoats and top hats – the boys still wear the tailcoats, but not the hats. Eton College is now the most famous public school in the country. A highlight of the year in Eton is the Procession of College Boats when crews from Eton College row along the Thames in vintage wooden boats, with the boys wearing hats decorated with flowers. The Procession originally took place on 4th June to commemorate the birthday of George III who had been a great patron of Eton College, but now takes place on the Wednesday before the first weekend of June.

One of the oldest buildings in Eton is number 47 High Street, dating back to 1420. Now a restaurant, the building used to be a pub called the Cock Pit, seen in photograph 81688, below, as it looked in 1929. Cock fights used to be held in the cock pit that still exists behind the building. Next to the building, and also seen in this photograph, is one of the oldest pillar boxes in the England, dating from 1856. It is a rare example of the earliest days of pillar box design, which were originally made with a vertical posting slot for the letters. However, it was soon realised that a vertical slot let in more rain, so the design was altered to have the horizontal posting slot that is the norm today.

Eton's High Street is linked to Windsor on the opposite bank of the Thames by an iron bridge built in the 1820s. Until 1897, there was a toll to cross the bridge – the living paid 2d to cross, while the departed could be carried across by coffin for 6/8d! This bridge was used by traffic until the 1970s, but is now only open to pedestrians and cyclists.

ETON, THE COCK PIT 1929 81688

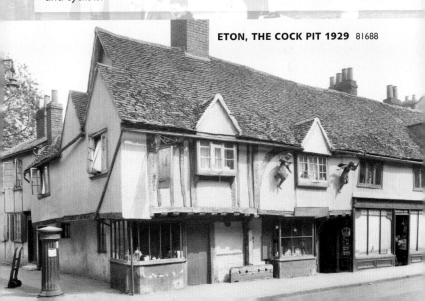

WINDSOR, THE CASTLE FROM THE RIVER 1895 35368A

Windsor is dominated by its famous castle, the principal residence of the sovereigns of the United Kingdom and the largest continually inhabited medieval castle in the world. Founded by William the Conqueror in the 11th century, the oldest parts of the present castle date from the 12th century, including the Round Tower – the building with the flagpole in photograph 35368a, above – but much of it dates from the 1820s, when King George IV spent a huge sum renovating and extending it. The magnificent building to the right of the castle precinct in the photograph is St George's Chapel, constructed between 1475 and 1528. The nave was completed in 1509 under the great master mason and architect William Vertue, who may be represented by the figure of a workman in the bottom right-hand pane of the great west window. St George's Chapel is the chapel of the Order of the Garter, the chivalric order founded by King Edward III in 1348, and the Knights' banners hang over its Quire stalls. The Order originally honoured knightly valour, but today's Knights of the Garter are chosen from people who have served their country notably, or achieved something exceptional.

Amongst the many items of interest to be seen in Windsor Castle are the bullet that killed Lord Nelson at the battle of Trafalgar in 1805, on display in the Grand Vestibule in the State Apartments, and a huge suit of armour that was made for King Henry VIII around 1540, seven years before he died, which gives an idea of the great size of the king in his final years – the suit measures 132cm (52 ins) around the waist, and stands at a height of 1.83 metres (6 feet).

The State Apartments of Windsor Castle are furnished with some of the finest artworks from the Royal Collection. One of the paintings on regular exhibition is the famous triple portrait of King Charles I that was painted in 1635 by Sir Anthony Van Dyck. Fourteen years later, in 1649 and following his defeat in the Civil War, King Charles I was executed by order of Parliament. A copy of the king's death warrant hangs on the exterior first floor wall of 7 Church Street in Windsor town.

The original town of Windsor was what is now Old Windsor, a few miles to the south-east, but the establishment of Windsor Castle caused a new town to develop around it that eventually eclipsed the earlier settlement in size and importance. The layout of medieval Windsor was very similar to that of today. There were two main streets, Peascod Street and Thames Street, coming up from the river and becoming the High Street and then Park Street. Peascod Street was named after the pea 'crofts', or pea fields, to which it led.

The area by the river at Windsor known as the Brocas is named after the Brocas family who owned the land in the 14th century and who lived in the nearby parish of Clewer.

The building of the handsome Guildhall in the centre of Windsor was completed by the famous architect Sir Christopher Wren (1632-1723) in 1689. The two baroque statues in niches on its exterior represent Queen Anne (1702-1714) and her husband, Prince George of Denmark; the statue of Prince George was presented in 1713 by Sir Christopher Wren's son, also called Christopher. Alongside the Guildhall (on the other side from this view) is a wonderfully crooked building that houses the Crooked House Tearoom (its correct name is Market Cross House). The house was built in 1687 with unseasoned timber which warped with the passage of time, causing the structure of the house to twist.

In the 17th century Nell Gwynn, the former orange seller who became a favourite mistress of King Charles II, lived in several houses around Windsor to be near the king when he was in residence in the castle. St Albans Street in the town is named after their eldest son Charles, who was created the Earl of Burford and Duke of St Albans; as the Dukes of St Albans, his descendants were prominent citizens in Windsor for many years.

WINDSOR, HIGH STREET AND THE GUILDHALL
1914 66987

WINDSOR, THE CASTLE 1914 66977

The statue of Queen Victoria at the junction of Castle Hill and Windsor's High Street commemorates her Golden Jubilee of 1887. Inside the plinth of the statue is a sealed Doulton jar containing every coin in circulation at that time.

At the south end of Windsor's High Street stands a pillar box painted blue. This is a special pillar box for airmail letters, in commemoration of the first airmail delivery of post in Britain, on 9th September 1911, when a delivery of post was flown from Hendon in north London to Windsor Great Park – a milestone in both aviation and postal history.

At the time of the First World War, in the reign of King George V, the British Royal Family was known by its 'house', or dynasty, of 'Saxe-Coburg-Gotha'. However, anti-German feeling during the war caused the Royal Family to look for a new name. King George loved Windsor Castle, so in 1917 the Royal Family adopted 'Windsor' not only as the new name for the Royal House, but also as the surname of the Royal Family.

ASCOT, HIGH STREET 1903 50690

A few miles south of Windsor is Ascot, situated in a wooded corner of the county that was once part of the ancient Windsor Forest, and famous for its racecourse. The Ascot Races were instituted by Queen Anne in 1711, and were originally run on Ascot Heath. The race course was moved to its present position in the 1740s by William, Duke of Cumberland (the second son of King George II), who was the first member of the Royal Family to be elected to the Jockey Club. In the early 20th century King Edward VII (1901-1910) did much to promote the Ascot races, and Ascot Week (or 'Royal Ascot') in June is now one of the key events on the social calendar, traditionally opened by the sovereign driving around the racecourse in an open carriage (as seen on the contents page of this book). The third day of Ascot Week is Gold Cup Day and is also known as 'Ladies Day', when in order to enter the Royal Enclosure all women must be wearing a hat that covers the 'crown of their head'. Ascot Ladies Day is now famous for the array of flamboyant and inventive hats that are created for the occasion.

West of Ascot is Bracknell, which grew up from the inns on the road between Ascot Heath and Reading, with coaches to and from London stopping there regularly. Most of the 'old' Bracknell has now been swept away and a new modern town has emerged, but one of the old inns from that time which still stands in modern Bracknell is the Bull Inn in the High Street, shown in photograph 46893 (below) as it appeared in 1901, bearing a sign advertising 'Good stabling'. In front of the Bull Inn nowadays is one of Bracknell's many fountains, featuring a large granite ball that rotates as it is suspended in a pool of water. Another of the town's water features is located nearby, in Charles Square, in the form of an unusual water clock. The middle ring of water jets represents the hours, and the outside ring represents the minutes. The water jets of the feature 'tell the time' every five minutes, then revert back to a random display in between.

BRACKNELL, HIGH STREET 1901 46893

Great changes came to Bracknell after it was chosen in 1948 to be the location of one of eight New Towns to be developed to solve the country's acute housing shortage following the Second World War. Bracknell New Town would provide homes for 25,000 new residents, mainly from Greater London, together with workplaces, shops and schools. The first of the initial four new 'neighbourhoods' to be developed was at Priestwood. The second new neighbourhood was at Easthampstead, and one of its landmark buildings, completed in 1964, was the 17-storey hexagonal tower block called Point Royal. This was an early building by the now-renowned architectural practice of Arup Associates, and was of much interest to avant-garde architects of the time. Even Nikolaus Pevsner described it as 'outstanding', in the Berkshire edition of his 'Buildings of England' of 1966. Much of Point Royal's support is derived from a central core, in which a lift is contained, providing access to the 102 apartments. Its contribution to architectural history has been recognised and it is now a Grade II listed building.

BRACKNELL, HIGH STREET 1901   46894x

38

EASTHAMPSTEAD, POINT ROYAL
c1965 E144018

Both Bracknell and nearby Wokingham were originally settlements in Windsor Forest, a large expanse of woodland and heathland. In the 18th century the area was terrorised by a gang of ruffians called the 'Wokingham Blacks' because they blackened their faces to disguise themselves. They began as poachers, but expanded into robbery, blackmail and murder. They were eventually captured, and a number were tried and hanged. As a result of their activities the 'Black Act' was passed in Parliament in 1723, making it a criminal offence to blacken one's face to commit unlawful acts, including poaching.

Wokingham became established as a market town in the 13th century, and its triangular market place remains the town's focal point, dominated by its Victorian Town Hall, also triangular in shape, that was erected in 1860 in Gothic revival style. The Town Hall also originally provided space for the County Police Station, with cells, an exercise yard, and a courtroom. Wokingham was known as 'Oakingham' in the past, meaning 'the town in the forest', which is why the coat of arms of Wokingham Borough Council features acorns and oak leaves.

WOKINGHAM, THE TOWN HALL 1906 57025

A significant number of medieval buildings survive in Wokingham, including the fine range of timber-framed houses in Rose Street seen in photograph W123014 (above). The tall narrow building second from the right in this view was once the premises of The Maiden School for girls, but from 1876 to 1921 it was the home of James Seaward, who served Wokingham as both a town councillor and an alderman but who is most famous in the town as the inspiration for the character of Tom, the boy chimney sweep in Charles Kingsley's classic children's book 'The Water Babies'. Born in a workhouse, James 'Sooty' Seaward was a chimney sweep by trade and swept the chimneys of Reverend Kingsley's rectory at Eversley, south of Wokingham. On his visits there he told the housekeeper about his childhood experiences as a 'climbing boy' apprenticed to a cruel chimney sweep. She in turn related them to Reverend Kingsley, which inspired the early part of the book. The connection is commemorated with a statue of two 'Water Babies' sitting on an open book by the entrance to Wokingham Library, installed in 1999.

South of Bracknell and Wokingham is Crowthorne. The Roman road called 'The Devil's Highway' passes through the village, which ran from London to the Roman town of 'Calleva Atrebatum' near Silchester, south of Reading. Crowthorne takes its name from a thorn tree that used to mark the junction of the Roman road and the Sandhurst to Bracknell Road, at what is now Brookers Corner. Crowthorne grew and developed mainly as a result of two institutions – Wellington College and Broadmoor Hospital – being built nearby in the mid 19th century. In the 1890s the name 'Albertonville' was suggested as an alternative name for the growing village, in honour of Prince Albert, husband of Queen Victoria, but this was successfully opposed by the residents.

Photograph 62895 (below) shows the main entrance to Broadmoor Asylum, which was built in an area of open heathland near Crowthorne in 1863. Originally called Broadmoor Criminal Lunatic Asylum, it became Broadmoor Institution in 1948, and is known today as Broadmoor Hospital, one of four special hospitals providing medical treatment of psychiatric patients under secure conditions.

CROWTHORNE, BROADMOOR ASYLUM ENTRANCE 1910 62895

FINCHAMPSTEAD, WELLINGTONIA AVENUE 1927 79647

Wellington College near Crowthorne is one of Britain's most famous public schools. Designed by the architect John Shaw, Wellington College opened to pupils in 1859. It was founded as a memorial to Arthur Wellesley, 1st Duke of Wellington, who was the victor of the battle of Waterloo in 1815. It was originally intended to provide schooling for the orphan sons of British Army officers, but in fact opened with a mixture of both orphaned boys and those with families.

Another link with the Duke of Wellington can be found west of Crowthorne, where there is a magnificent avenue of 110 huge Wellingtonia trees along the B3348 road towards Finchampstead. The photograph on this page shows the trees as they appeared in 1927 – they are considerably taller now. They were planted in 1863 as a commemoration of the Duke, whose home was at nearby Strathfield Saye, just over the county border in Hampshire. Wellingtonia trees (more correctly called Giant Sequoias, or Sierra Redwoods) were introduced to Britain in 1853 and were named 'Wellingtonia Gigantea' by John Lindley in honour of the Duke of Wellington, who had died the year before.

43

SANDHURST, ST MICHAEL'S CHURCH, THE INTERIOR c1955 S56016

South of Crowthorne and close to the Surrey border is Sandhurst. One of Sandhurst's most famous buildings is its church of St Michael. The first church on this site dated back to 1220, but in 1853 its rector began a rebuilding programme. The new south aisle, tower and spire, and east and west ends were completed rebuilt in sandstone, designed by G E Street, in an Early English style. The design of the Norman-style doorway in the porch entrance of the south-west tower may have been based on an original. The font is Norman in style too, said to have been 'executed by one of the daughters of the late rector'. Twelve years later, a new north aisle and the chancel meant that the old church had been completely replaced. The wall paintings inside the church (dating from 1880) are striking, and the monuments include a memorial of 1892 in Athenian style to Lady Farrer. A Jacobean brass of 1608 is also noteworthy.

In the 1820s the Sandhurst estate in Berkshire was chosen as the location for a new Royal Military College for the training of army officers. The original RMC College building was designed in neo-classical style by one of the leading architects of the day, James Wyatt. It is now known as the Old College of the Royal Military Academy, Sandhurst, and is shown in photograph S56710 (below). It is one of Berkshire's most distinguished landmark buildings. Its handsome portico plays an important part in the passing out parade (properly known as the Sovereign's Parade) when officer cadets graduate from the RMA. The officer cadets about to be awarded their commissions march in slow time up the steps to the strains of 'Auld Lang Syne', and the parade is then concluded by the Academy Adjutant riding his horse up the steps behind them. The brass cannon on each side of the steps were used at the battle of Waterloo in 1815.

SANDHURST, THE OLD COLLEGE 2004 S56710

SPORTING BERKSHIRE

Berkshire is noted for several important race courses, the most famous of which is Ascot, which hosts 9 of the UK's 32 annual Group 1 races. The most prestigious race run at Ascot is the King George VI and Queen Elizabeth Stakes in July, but the most famous event there is probably the Royal Meeting in June, also known as Ascot Week, the highlight of which is the Gold Cup, open to thoroughbreds aged four years or older and run over a distance of 2 miles and 4 furlongs (4,023 metres). The Gold Cup is Britain's most prestigious event for 'stayers' – those horses which specialise in racing over long distances – and is the first leg of Britain's 'Stayers' Triple Crown' – the second leg is the Goodwood Cup and, and the third is the Doncaster Cup. Many top races, both flat and National Hunt, are run at Newbury racecourse, which celebrated its 100th anniversary in 2005; one of the most popular is always the Hennessy Gold Cup, a steeplechase run in late November or early December. Royal Windsor Racecourse is one of only two figure-of-eight courses in the UK, and was voted the 'best small racecourse in the South East' by members of The Racegoers Club in 2010. Flat racing takes place there 26 times a year from April to October.

Royal Windsor Horse Show is Britain's largest outdoor equestrian show, and has been staged every May since 1943. Originally it was Windsor Horse and Dog Show and the aim was to raise money for the war effort. The Royal Family attended the show and Princess Elizabeth (later to be Queen Elizabeth II) won the Pony and Dogcart Class. Windsor also hosts the Windsor International Horse Trials in Windsor Great Park every May, which is one of the biggest events in the equestrian calendar.

Reading Football Club is Berkshire's only professional football club. They were formerly nicknamed 'The Biscuit Men' because of the Huntley & Palmer biscuits works that used to be in the town, but are now known as 'The Royals', due to the town's location in the Royal County of Berkshire. Since 1998 they have been based in the 24,084-capacity Madejski stadium, which is named after the chairman, John Madejski. Reading Football Club hold two notable records. In 1985/86 they won their first 13 games in Division Three. This is still the record for the most consecutive wins at the beginning of the League season in any division. They also hold the record for the longest run without conceding a goal. In 1978/79 they went for 1,074 minutes without conceding a goal, including 11 complete matches. Steve Death was the goalkeeper throughout the 11 games. Reading's Madejski stadium is also the venue for the home games of the Aviva Premiership rugby union team London Irish RFC.

Newbury Rugby Club was founded as far back as 1928. However, the club's greatest successes have come in recent times. One spectacular season was 1996/97, when the first team won National Division 4 South with a 100% win record.

Sunningdale Golf Club in east Berkshire was founded in 1900, and its Ladies Golf Club is the oldest in the country. The course is famous for the beauty of its setting, and is a favourite with many golf professionals. The famous crime author Agatha Christie lived in the Sunningdale area in the 1920s and the Sunningdale golf course featured in one of her short stories, titled 'The Sunningdale Mystery', first published in 1929.

Situated as it is on the River Thames, it is not surprising that Maidenhead is a rowing centre. The Maidenhead Rowing Club hosts the Maidenhead Regatta every August, which attracts top crews from around the UK and is seen as one of the major testing regattas for Olympic hopefuls.

QUIZ QUESTIONS

Answers on page 52.

1. At Inkpen Hill in the southernmost corner of south-western Berkshire, south of Hungerford and Kintbury, the bare, open spaces of the Berkshire Downs reach 954 feet (291 metres) above sea level, and nearby Walbury Hill reaches 974 feet (297 metres), making this not only the highest point of Berkshire but also the highest point of any chalk downs in the South East of England. Walbury Hill is the start point for two long distance footpaths, the Test Way and the Wayfarers Walk. What grisly reminder of crime and punishment in the past can be found beside the Test Way on the downs adjacent to Walbury Hill, between the villages of Inkpen and Combe?

2. According to the 'Guinness Book of Records', the shortest street in England is in a Berkshire town – where is it?

3. What item of clothing is named after the Berkshire town of Eton?

4. What is the name for an inhabitant of Maidenhead?

5. What are known as 'the Aldworth Giants', and whereabouts in Berkshire can you find them?

6. Speenhamland is a district between the centre of Newbury and the village of Speen, to the north of the River Kennet. The notorious 'Speenhamland System' originated there in 1795. What was this?

7. What sports are played by the Bracknell Bees and the Bracknell Blazers, respectively?

8. What colour is the Berkshire breed of pig?

9. Two famous products that are household names are linked with Slough. According to their advertising slogans, one will help you 'work, rest and play' all day, and then the other will help you recover and 'unwind for a good night's sleep'. What are they?

10. The area now known as Forbury Gardens in Reading was bought by the Council in the 1850s to be laid out as a public park. In Forbury Gardens is one of Reading's most famous landmarks, the Maiwand Memorial (see photograph 27139, below). This extraordinary monument is dominated by a colossal cast iron lion weighing 16 tons, believed to be the world's largest lion statue. The lion is so associated with Reading that it even appears on the badge of Reading Football Club – but what does it commemorate?

READING, THE MAIWAND MEMORIAL 1890 27139

RECIPE

BERKSHIRE HOG

Berkshire is famous for the quality of its pork. A local breed of pig is the Berkshire Pig, which was developed in the 18th century. It declined in popularity in the 20th century because the breed is slow-maturing and the meat was not lean enough for modern tastes, but in recent years there has been renewed interest in the Berkshire Pig and its fine, well-flavoured meat. This is the pork to seek out at good butchers and farmers' markets if you want to serve up a joint of roast pork with proper crispy crackling – you need that old-fashioned layer of fat on the meat to make really good crackling.

> 4 pork chops, wiped and trimmed
> 300ml/ ½ pint white wine or good stock
> 150ml/ ¼ pint single cream
> 115g/4oz mushrooms, wiped and sliced
> 1 tablespoonful oil
> 25g/1oz butter
> 8 shallots or very small onions, peeled
> 1 bouquet garni
> 1 tablespoonful plain flour
> Salt and freshly ground black pepper

Heat the butter and oil in a frying pan. Add the pork chops and lightly brown them on each side. Remove the pork chops, add the sliced onions to the pan and gently cook until golden. Add the wine or stock and the bouquet garni. Return the pork chops to the frying pan, bring the liquid to the boil, cover and simmer gently for 45-50 minutes. Add the sliced mushrooms and cook for 10 minutes.

Mix the flour with a little of the cream. Remove the pan from the heat and carefully stir in the flour and cream mixture. Return the pan to the heat, bring to the boil and boil for one minute, stirring all the time. Add the remainder of the cream, stirring well to heat through, but do not allow it to boil. Remove the bouquet garni, adjust the seasoning and serve.

RECIPE

POOR KNIGHTS OF WINDSOR

In 1349 King Edward III founded an order of military pensioners at Windsor known as the 'Poor Knights', whose job it was to pray for the souls of the Knights of the Garter (see page 32) in return for relief and comfortable sustenance. It was Henry VIII's daughter Mary Tudor, who reigned as Queen Mary I from 1553-1558, who had a row of almshouses built into the south wall of Windsor Castle for the Poor Knights to live in (made from stone 'recycled' from Reading Abbey). These houses are inhabited nowadays by the Military Knights, the successors to the Poor Knights. One of the houses is in the Mary Tudor Tower, on which can be seen the coat of arms of Mary Tudor and her husband Philip II of Spain, the only example in the country. No one knows how this simple recipe came to be called after the 'Poor Knights', but it makes a deliciously rich but economical dessert that belies its name. It is a good way of using slightly stale, leftover bread. This makes enough for 4 people.

> 4 slices of stale white bread with their crusts removed
> 1 tablespoonful of caster sugar
> 150ml/5 fl oz milk
> 1 tablespoonful of sherry
> 4 egg yolks, beaten
> 75g/3oz butter
> 1 teaspoonful of ground cinnamon
> A red jam of choice – strawberry, raspberry, bramble, damson etc

Dissolve the sugar in the milk in a shallow dish, and add the sherry. Cut each slice of bread in half, and dip each half into the milk mixture, and then into the beaten egg yolks to coat them. Melt the butter in a wide frying pan, and fry the bread pieces a few at a time until they are golden brown on both sides. Drain each piece as it has been cooked, and keep hot until all the slices have been fried. Sprinkle the fried bread slices generously with sugar and cinnamon and serve whilst they are still hot, spread with jam.

QUIZ ANSWERS

1. At the top of Gallows Down between the villages of Inkpen and Combe is a gibbet (grid reference SU36020). It is a replica of the structure that was erected there in 1676 for the purpose of gibbeting the bodies of George Broomham and Dorothy Newman, a pair of lovers who were hanged for murdering George's wife and son. The original gibbet was destroyed many years ago but a replica has been kept on the site ever since, as a warning and deterrent to others.

2. Charlotte Street in Windsor, the little street running down the side of the Crooked House Tearoom (properly Market Cross House) is named after Queen Charlotte, the wife of King George III, and is listed in the 'Guinness Book of Records' as the shortest street in England at 51 feet and 10 inches (16 metres) long.

3. The Eton collar – a wide stiff buttoned white collar worn over the lapels of a jacket that forms part of the uniform of Eton College. It became a fashionable clothing item for young boys in the 19th century.

4. The name for an inhabitant of Maidenhead is a 'Maidonian'.

5. In the north of Berkshire is Aldworth, off the B4009 road between Newbury and Streatley. Inside its parish church of St Mary the Virgin are a number of monuments to members of the De La Beche family who in medieval times lived at a fortified manor at Aldworth that stood on the site of what is now Beche Farm. The effigies are supposed to be life-sized representations, but as a number of them depict knights who are over seven feet long, they have been dubbed 'the Aldworth Giants'.

6. The Pelican Inn at Speenhamland was the setting in 1795 for a meeting of Berkshire magistrates where the infamous Speenhamland System was devised. This was a way of calculating the amount of relief paid to the poor from local parish rates by tying the amount of relief payments to the cost of a loaf of bread, according to family size and the level of local wages. The Speenhamland System came to be used all over England, but was much criticised as it resulted in employers deliberately keeping wages at a low level, knowing that the difference would be made up by people being forced to undergo the humiliation of applying for assistance from the parish.

7. The Bracknell Bees play ice hockey in the English Premier League. The Bracknell Blazers play British basketball in the British Basketball Federation National League.

8. The Berkshire Pig is black, often with white on the legs, face and tip of the tail.

9. Mars Bars and Horlicks. The Mars Bar was developed by an American called Forrest Mars in his confectionary business on the Slough Estate in 1932. The Slough factory now makes a staggering three million Mars Bars a day! The Horlicks malted milk drink was first made in Slough in 1908 after James Horlick opened his purpose-built redbrick factory on Stoke Poges Lane near Slough railway station. The factory is still a local landmark, although now owned by GlaxoSmithKline, and Horlicks continues to be manufactured there.

10. The Maiwand Memorial in Reading was erected in the 1880s to commemorate eleven officers and 318 other ranks of the 66th (Berkshire) Regiment who died in the Second Afghan War of 1879-80, particularly for their rearguard action at Maiwand in Afghanistan.

FRANCIS FRITH

PIONEER VICTORIAN PHOTOGRAPHER

Francis Frith, founder of the world-famous photographic archive, was a complex and multi-talented man. A devout Quaker and a highly successful Victorian businessman, he was philosophical by nature and pioneering in outlook. By 1855 he had already established a wholesale grocery business in Liverpool, and sold it for the astonishing sum of £200,000, which is the equivalent today of over £15,000,000. Now in his thirties, and captivated by the new science of photography, Frith set out on a series of pioneering journeys up the Nile and to the Near East.

INTRIGUE AND EXPLORATION

He was the first photographer to venture beyond the sixth cataract of the Nile. Africa was still the mysterious 'Dark Continent', and Stanley and Livingstone's historic meeting was a decade into the future. The conditions for picture taking confound belief. He laboured for hours in his wicker dark-room in the sweltering heat of the desert, while the volatile chemicals fizzed dangerously in their trays. Back in London he exhibited his photographs and was 'rapturously cheered' by members of the Royal Society. His reputation as a photographer was made overnight.

VENTURE OF A LIFE-TIME

By the 1870s the railways had threaded their way across the country, and Bank Holidays and half-day Saturdays had been made obligatory by Act of Parliament. All of a sudden the working man and his family were able to enjoy days out, take holidays, and see a little more of the world.

With typical business acumen, Francis Frith foresaw that these new tourists would enjoy having souvenirs to commemorate their days out. For the next thirty years he travelled the country by train and by pony and trap, producing fine photographs of seaside resorts and beauty spots that were keenly bought by millions of Victorians. These prints were painstakingly pasted into family albums and pored over during the dark nights of winter, rekindling precious memories of summer excursions. Frith's studio was soon supplying retail shops all over the country, and by 1890 F Frith & Co had become the greatest specialist photographic publishing company in the world, with over 2,000 sales outlets, and pioneered the picture postcard.

FRANCIS FRITH'S LEGACY

Francis Frith had died in 1898 at his villa in Cannes, his great project still growing. By 1970 the archive he created contained over a third of a million pictures showing 7,000 British towns and villages.

Frith's legacy to us today is of immense significance and value, for the magnificent archive of evocative photographs he created provides a unique record of change in the cities, towns and villages throughout Britain over a century and more. Frith and his fellow studio photographers revisited locations many times down the years to update their views, compiling for us an enthralling and colourful pageant of British life and character.

We are fortunate that Frith was dedicated to recording the minutiae of everyday life. For it is this sheer wealth of visual data, the painstaking chronicle of changes in dress, transport, street layouts, buildings, housing and landscape that captivates us so much today, offering us a powerful link with the past and with the lives of our ancestors.

Computers have now made it possible for Frith's many thousands of images to be accessed almost instantly. The archive offers every one of us an opportunity to examine the places where we and our families have lived and worked down the years. Its images, depicting our shared past, are now bringing pleasure and enlightenment to millions around the world a century and more after his death.

For further information visit: www.francisfrith.com

INTERIOR DECORATION

Frith's photographs can be seen framed and as giant wall murals in thousands of pubs, restaurants, hotels, banks, retail stores and other public buildings throughout Britain. These provide interesting and attractive décor, generating strong local interest and acting as a powerful reminder of gentler days in our increasingly busy and frenetic world.

FRITH PRODUCTS

All Frith photographs are available as prints and posters in a variety of different sizes and styles. In the UK we also offer a range of other gift and stationery products illustrated with Frith photographs, although many of these are not available for delivery outside the UK – see our web site for more information on the products available for delivery in your country.

THE INTERNET

Over 100,000 photographs of Britain can be viewed and purchased on the Frith web site. The web site also includes memories and reminiscences contributed by our customers, who have personal knowledge of localities and of the people and properties depicted in Frith photographs. If you wish to learn more about a specific town or village you may find these reminiscences fascinating to browse. Why not add your own comments if you think they would be of interest to others? See **www.francisfrith.com**

PLEASE HELP US BRING FRITH'S PHOTOGRAPHS TO LIFE

Our authors do their best to recount the history of the places they write about. They give insights into how particular towns and villages developed, they describe the architecture of streets and buildings, and they discuss the lives of famous people who lived there. But however knowledgeable our authors are, the story they tell is necessarily incomplete.

Frith's photographs are so much more than plain historical documents. They are living proofs of the flow of human life down the generations. They show real people at real moments in history; and each of those people is the son or daughter of someone, the brother or sister, aunt or uncle, grandfather or grandmother of someone else. All of them lived, worked and played in the streets depicted in Frith's photographs.

We would be grateful if you would give us your insights into the places shown in our photographs: the streets and buildings, the shops, businesses and industries. Post your memories of life in those streets on the Frith website: what it was like growing up there, who ran the local shop and what shopping was like years ago; if your workplace is shown tell us about your working day and what the building is used for now. Read other visitors' memories and reconnect with your shared local history and heritage. With your help more and more Frith photographs can be brought to life, and vital memories preserved for posterity, and for the benefit of historians in the future.

Wherever possible, we will try to include some of your comments in future editions of our books. Moreover, if you spot errors in dates, titles or other facts, please let us know, because our archive records are not always completely accurate—they rely on 140 years of human endeavour and hand-compiled records. You can email us using the contact form on the website.

Thank you!

For further information, trade, or author enquiries
please contact us at the address below:

**The Francis Frith Collection, Oakley Business Park,
Wylye Road, Dinton, Wiltshire SP3 5EU.**
Tel: +44 (0)1722 716 376 Fax: +44 (0)1722 716 881
e-mail: sales@francisfrith.co.uk **www.francisfrith.com**